AMAZING WINTER OLYMPICS

ICE HOCKEY

BY ASHLEY GISH

CREATIVE EDUCATION • CREATIVE PAPE

Published by Creative Education and Creative Paperbacks
P.O. Box 227, Mankato, Minnesota 56002
Creative Education and Creative Paperbacks are imprints of
The Creative Company
www.thecreativecompany.us

Design by The Design Lab
Production by Rachel Klimpel
Art direction by Rita Marshall
Printed in the United States of America

Photographs by Alamy (ITAR-TASS News Agency, PCN Photogra-
phy, REUTERS, Stefan Sollfors, ZUMA Press), AP Images (ASSOCI-
ATED PRESS), Dreamstime (Zhukovsky), Getty Images (ullstein bild/
ullstein bild), iStockphoto (AndrewJohnson, Shell_114), Shutterstock
(Mike Flippo, katatonia82, Robert Nyholm, Adam Vilimek)

Library of Congress Cataloging-in-Publication Data
Names: Gish, Ashley, author.
Title: Ice hockey / Ashley Gish.
Series: Amazing Winter Olympics.
Includes bibliographical references and index.
Summary: Celebrate the Winter Games with this high-interest intro-
duction to ice hockey, the team sport known for its pucks and sticks.
Also included is a historical story about Women's Team USA.

Identifiers:
ISBN 978-1-64026-496-0 (hardcover)
ISBN 978-1-68277-048-1 (pbk)
ISBN 978-1-64000-626-3 (eBook)
This title has been submitted for CIP processing under LCCN
2021937892.

Table of Contents

People began playing ice hockey in the early 1800s. It became Canada's national sport in 1880. Men's ice hockey debuted at the Summer Olympics in 1920. It moved to the first Winter Olympic Games in 1924. A women's event was added in 1998.

Canada won the gold medal at the 1920 Olympics in Antwerp, Belgium.

Team USA's win over the Soviet Union in 1980 was called the "Miracle on Ice."

Canada won the gold medal at many early Winter Olympics. From 1956 to 1988, the Soviet Union dominated the sport. The United States won in 1960 and again in 1980.

Soviet Union the name for the country of Russia from 1922 to 1991

The International Olympic Committee organizes events that decide which teams will compete at the Winter Games. Twelve men's teams and eight women's teams play at the Games.

International Olympic Committee the group of people in charge of organizing the Summer and Winter Olympic Games; the group is based in Switzerland

Two teams compete in each match.

Each match has three 20-minute periods. Players take a 15-minute break after the first and second periods.

Before they make it to the Olympics, the best teams in the world must play against each other.

Each team has 20 players. Coaches, trainers, and captains work with the team. During the game, six players from each team can be on the ice at once. There are three offensive players, two defensive players, and one goalie.

An Olympic ice rink is wider than rinks used for professional North American games.

Offensive players try to

score a goal. They hit the **puck** into the other team's net. Defensive players try to keep the other team from scoring goals. The goalie guards the net.

puck a small rubber disk used to score goals in ice hockey

Players wear helmets and padded gear. Mouthguards protect their teeth. Goalies wear a mask and thicker pads. Players wear skates, too. They block shots with their skates.

Skates' sharp blades dig into the ice, helping players make tight turns.

Pucks are frozen before each game so that they will slide more and bounce less on the ice.

blade

They use hockey sticks to shoot, pass, and carry the puck. Many sticks are made from fiberglass or aluminum. The thin end of the stick is called the blade. Players control the puck with the blade.

fiberglass a strong material made from a mix of glass and plastic fibers

Ice hockey players zoom back and forth across the ice. They pass the puck to each other. Then they shoot it at the goal. Catch the action of this exciting sport at the next Winter Olympic Games.

Both Canada and the United States have been strong competitors in women's ice hockey.

Competitor Spotlight: Women's Team USA

In 1998, the Olympics featured women's hockey for the first time. Team USA took gold that year. For the next four Winter Olympics, Canada came in first. In 2018, the USA faced off against Canada for the gold medal. The game went into overtime. A shootout went on for six rounds. Finally, Jocelyne Lamoureux-Davidson scored the winning shot. Team USA women's ice hockey had its first gold medal in 20 years!

Read More

Herman, Gail. *What Is the Stanley Cup?* New York: Penguin Workshop, 2019.

Monson, James. *Behind the Scenes Hockey.* Minneapolis: Lerner, 2020.

Page, Sam. *Hockey: Then to WOW!* New York: Liberty Street, 2017.

Websites

DKFindout!: Ice Hockey
https://www.dkfindout.com/us/sports/ice-hockey/
Learn more about ice hockey gear.

Iconic Ice Hockey Players at the Olympics
https://www.youtube.com/watch?v=NGIho7rZZf0
Watch exciting moments in ice hockey at the Winter Olympics.

Note: Every effort has been made to ensure that the websites listed above are suitable for children, that they have educational value, and that they contain no inappropriate material. However, because of the nature of the Internet, it is impossible to guarantee that these sites will remain active indefinitely or that their contents will not be altered.

Index